MW00467271

Five-year-old In A Box: A True Love Story

By Lateshia Simpson

Publisher: MAWMedia Group

© 2020 Lateshia Simpson

First Edition: March 2020

Five-year-old In A Box: A True Love Story/ Lateshia Simpson

ISBN: 978-1-943616-33-6

MAWMedia Group, LLC
www.mawmedia.com
Reno, NV   Los Angeles, CA   Nashville, TN

ABOUT ME

Lateshia Simpson was born and raised in Charleston SC. In 2018, the mother of four and grandmother lost her husband to heart failure

and moved to Georgia to focus on what was next to come. As an introspective motivational author, she takes us through interwoven stories of heartbreak, lost dreams, hardship, and breakthrough in this book titled

Five-Year-Old In A Box: A True Love Story

Lateshia captivates us by sharing insightful experiences effectively to engage readers at multiple levels. This inspirational book on courage, resilience, and perseverance provides a master blueprint for overcoming obstacles and setbacks to mature into the woman you are meant to become.

Table of Contents

Section I: Five Years Old.. 7

Chapter 1: Five Forever.. 8

Chapter 2: The Ugly Duckling..15

Chapter 3: Love of a Father 22

Chapter 4: Finding My Father......................................28

Section II: Meeting My Father....................................34

Chapter 5: Leaving 35

Chapter 6: Cooper's Bridge 44

Chapter 7: Letting Go of Father..................................54

Section III: Loving Myself...59

Chapter 8: Finding Myself in Loss...............................60

Chapter 9: Deeper into God..69

Chapter 10: Finding My Peace....................................73

Section I: Five Years Old

Chapter 1: Five Forever

There is no feeling like being trapped in your own body. Not able to get help or help yourself. On the outside, I was developing just fine. But on the inside my very soul was slipping away. It wasn't until I was in my late 30s that I realized how on the verge of suicide I was. I needed help. My search to find someone professional to talk to started on the internet. After reviewing the pictures and reading several profiles and about what each provider offered, I finally choose a psychiatrist from the list. Though I knew I was doing the right thing, something inside me was afraid. It took all I had to make the call. I needed things to change because if they didn't, I didn't have much time left.

The woman on the other end of the phone sounded friendly. She asked me some questions from her over-the-phone assessment form. Already on overload I tried to be as patient as I could. I know the woman was just taking the time to get me the help that I needed. When she asked why I called and how I felt at that moment I wanted to scream out about every abuse I had experienced. It wasn't time for that. Then she asked me how soon I needed to be seen.

"As soon as possible was my response," was my immediate response. I was suicidal for years and even then, I felt bits of me fading away. I had reached my breaking point.

My appointment was set, but I was still anxious about discussing my issues with someone and more anxious about what they would tell me to do to fix it for myself. I don't know that I had the capacity to do it. My motivation was my kids. I needed to get a handle on me before it affected them. They say kids can feel when you are overwhelmed. They didn't deserve to feel what I was feeling.

The day of my appointment I drove slowly. I don't know why exactly. Maybe it was the speaking with someone. I think I was afraid of what would be released when I started remembering things. To my surprise the psychiatrist made me feel comfortable. Our session lasted about an hour. Speaking with her made me feel like I could have talked to anyone. I talked about the abuse and how it made me feel trapped. I have always felt like I was still holding on to that 5-year old girl inside of me. I told her that. After a while the psychiatrist provided a response.

"That five-year-old is trying to take care of you," she said.

I released to that understanding. Things were locked away inside of me, I felt the pressure often. That's why I needed to talk with someone. After our talk I continued to see the 5-year-old girl every time I got upset.

I call where I keep her "The Box." When I start to get upset and cry, I noticed how I kept her in the box. I would scream and have all these emotions, but I didn't hear myself. No one could hear me. I could see her screaming in the box, but there was nothing I could do. I didn't see a way to release her. We were both uncapable of helping each other. There I was an adult and a child. The 5-year-old girl inside me did her best to provide some relief, by screaming. I could feel the pressure, but unable to feel the release.

The feeling reminds me of the times I would go to church. I started to attend the church of my biological family. They would sing and it felt like water started at my feet and steadily rose through my body until it reached my head. Each time I felt it, I'd stop the feeling by running out of the church. The people there would say you need to release it and leave it at the altar. I don't know what made me run out. I think now, I must have been afraid of the release. There was so much hurt inside me that it was scary to see what it looked like coming out. In my mind, I thought it was safer inside where no one could see it, not even me.

In my family, I have an older sister, a younger sister, a mom and dad. When I was younger, my father was fireman. Later, he was a factory worker. My mom was a crossing guard for over twenty years. My father was physically abusive, and my mom was always the type to put him before us. There was a point when the abuse switched from my mom to us. I am not comfortable showing emotion because of how my father would not allow us to cry when he abused us. My mother did not have a voice. Whatever my father said, that was it. When the abuse turned from her to us, she said nothing. If we cried, we would get hit more. It's funny how people can go out in public with a smile on their face, and never know what is going on in the home. We always had welts from the extension cords. My father knew exactly where to hit our legs and back. I was taught that being disciplined is the result of a need for correction. Kids in the neighborhood knew what was going on. There were days when we had to run to the next house because we were being abused. My father seemed to be angry with my mother all the time for whatever reason. I just believed that we were not good kids. We would stay in our rooms all the time. If we left toys on the floor, we would get beat for it. He would put force behind his hit.

My mother and father had known each other since they were little kids. They grew up together. They went to school together. I don't know what their relationship was like then. I only remember that my sisters and I were constantly going back and forth to my aunt's house to get away. I was about 10-years-old when my baby sister arrived. The only thing that changed was she was spoiled rotten. Everything that my older sister and I wanted, was presented to her. My mom was pregnant another time with boys. Things didn't turn out well. The boys lived 3 months in the hospital 2 separate times, before they passed away. Since my parents owned the home, we grew up in, we were always remodeling it. My sisters and I had to tear down walls and strip the floors. I think my father wanted boys badly. He treated us girls like boys.

It is a struggle to remember any good days. I do remember us going to Disney World once per year. We went for about six years straight. We had fun there. Somewhere during that time my cousins began staying with my grandmother until my grandmother's husband passed away. Then they all came to live with my mother. I was 16 when my little cousins came to live with us. Our small two-bedroom house had transformed into a 5-bedroom house by the time I was 17. Up to the time that I moved away, my mother had custody of my aunt's three children. My cousins were spared the abuse that we had to go through. I figured it was because they weren't my parent's actual kids and money was involved. Anyone who came into the home would leave disturbed. That's how it is.

I don't know the words to describe what my feelings are toward my mother. My sisters and I would ask her why she allowed us to be so abused. She didn't have an answer. I feel she was afraid the abuse would switch back to her. I think my mom felt like she carried out her responsibility as a mother; she raised us, fed us, clothed us, and gave us shelter. Those are things that you must do as a mother, though I would also add safety and the feeling of being loved. My parents never told us they loved us. No hugs. No statement of, "I'm proud of you." We never received those kinds of things.

Only in our fantasy world could we think about going to go to our mother for help whenever we needed it. But our reality never went like that. We never went to my mother for anything. If we slipped and asked for something it would be shared with my father. Then we would hear about it the next day in an argument.

The only thing that gave me hope was waiting to be old enough to live my life in my own way. I didn't know how I was going to survive, but I knew I was going to make it somehow. My parents were always arguing. We got to the point of just trying to tune it out and stay out of my father's way. To this day, my relationship with my mom is still a work in progress. Now that I'm taking care of her long-distance, I'm doing what I can to build something from there.

The 5-year-old girl in the box had so much to carry around. The years of abuse had taken its toll on her. When my husband died, I finally released her. During that time, I got on my knees and began praying so hard, "God take me and not him!" The water started flowing like a river from my eyes. This time I heard the 5-year-old girl screaming. It was my nurturing coming out. Regardless of how our marriage was, I would trade my life for his. Even though he pushed me away, he wanted me there. I was always there. My life wasn't perfect, but I wanted to take the specter of death away from him.

Chapter 2: The Ugly Duckling

Have you ever felt like you were living a life that you didn't deserve? That's exactly how I felt. I had questions. Things just didn't measure up for me. I looked at the family I was raised with and noticed that I was different. As time went on, I gained clarity and things started making sense. The reason I was treated differently and looked different than anyone in my family was no longer just a fragment of my imagination. I found out that the man that raised me was not my biological father. There was another family out there that I came from and never knew.

Different

Being different raised more questions for me than what I looked like. There was also the question of love. The abuse I experienced from the father that raised me left a scar far deeper than the ones that showed up on my back, legs and arms. Then there was my mother who chose not to get involved. As a young adult trying to live life outside of that experience, I needed something I was never nurtured in. I looked in the mirror and didn't like what I saw. I have strong features. There was no resemblance between me and my sister, my mother, or father who raised me. I didn't look like anyone on either side of the family. It's one thing to not look like your family but I didn't feel like I belonged either. I felt like a victim of circumstance and no one felt they owed me anything, not even love. I was glad to grow up and leave home. I just never figured the hurt I experienced would be so hard to recover from. That's what I learned; things don't just go away because your life has changed. Hurt and pain must be addressed before you can let it go.

I'm still learning how to love myself. I saw a woman one time who said, "You are so beautiful." It's hard to see what other people see. While that woman was seeing how beautiful I was on the outside, she had no idea of the life I had lived. She didn't realize the struggle I went through every day to believe in myself enough to perform the task right before me. Her words didn't land on fertile ground. You never know what is going on in a person's head. They may be the most beautiful person, but they may not feel that way. I take a lot of pictures. That's how I attempt to learn about myself.

Loving myself was a process that began with me loving God first. I needed to believe in something bigger than myself. Whatever I learned I held on to it and allowed it to nurture my spirit. I would pray and ask God to send people into my life that were positive. I wanted God to send me someone who could love me unconditionally. For once I wanted to be put first. But I realized that I first had to understand how to love and give what I wanted. This caused me to study my bible more to understand it fully.

I had to learn who I was in the different roles I held, as a woman, a mother, and a wife. When I was married my husband became ill. Watching him go through what he did taught me to value my life. Every day I cherish the life I have been given. I don't take life for granted; I enjoy it to the fullest. Though I have met some challenges in my life I have always been family oriented, putting family first.

Family Matters

Not having the best family life growing up didn't stop me from loving those around me. I have always been the type of person who tried to see the good in people. I was surprised whenever someone proved me wrong. I would hear people say negative things about me or throw shade (To say rude things or publicly criticize another person). Things came to the light for me when my family members and friends began to come to me with things that others had said.

My heart immediately sank. Hearing mean words that every-body had been telling me about is one thing. Witnessing it for myself was another. I heard the most hurtful things along with calling me every bad name in the book. My first response was to defend myself, but I never spoke. Deep in my heart I knew it would've done any good. People who hurt, hurt others. I saw a person hurting badly. I tried to think of what I might have done to make someone feel the way about me. But nothing came to mind. I realized that I must give some rela-tionships to God. My love is not the cure, the problem is not me. I am at a point where I must be better without toxic people in my life.

Compliments like beautiful and gorgeous always seemed to come my way. I even think I'm cute but when did that become a prob-lem. I found out that I was from another family and animosity for me intensified. Being different should not cause hate in others. Regard-less of the hate I had to feel good about myself in some way. I always keep my face done up and myself together. My life is mine, I don't share much. I enjoy my privacy.

Some members of the family are not driven. They smoke, drink, and sit around doing nothing. I was riding with a family member once and she stated, "You think you are all that." How does one re-spond to such a statement? No one knows the severity of what I have gone through. Depression, anxiety, suicidal ideation, no one knew that side of me. I am realizing that some, even in my family, don't know my story. How am I loved by so many others outside of my family? I am faulted for wanting more. Some of my family fault me for being the best I can be. Finally, I can do many of the things that I have wanted to. This puts me in a mode of appreciation. I appreciate my husband because everything that he did not do while he was living, he has done in death. He has put me in a position to build my life the way I can build my life. Before husband died, I gave all of myself to him. After he was gone, I initially felt lost. If I wasn't helping with something, I didn't feel whole. I am grateful for the push my friends gives to make me realize that I am different. I own that difference. It is not a curse, but a blessing. I want more out of life. It's okay to be different. God made each of us special in our own way. You must only own it. Everyone is put here for different reasons. You must find your purpose in life. It's a sad truth to realize that leaving and not being around my family makes me better. I flourish and can enjoy an environment outside of the negativity.

Church Solace

The web of pain stretches in every direction. One hurt lead to another hurt. The cycle continues unless someone with enough courage breaks it. The church my mother attended was where she met my biological father. They attended that church for years. The father that raised me attended the same church, but he wasn't involved much.

He attended different churches. My stepfather and mother were dating since they were young. They were in gospel groups together. My stepfather was abusive to my mom. He drove my mom to seek comfort from another man, my biological father.

Finding out pieces of my mom's story brings more clarity to my experience. Every time my stepfather looked at me, I must have reminded him of something terrible, a betrayal he couldn't forgive. Yet, I was not the cause of the problem only the result of a consequence. But I paid the price for it anyway. I also learned that the church we attended was my grandfather's church, my biological father's father. It was the only place that my biological father said he saw me. I remember people coming to see me at home, but I don't know whether he really knew I wasn't the child of the man in my home. My mom never came out and told him.

After going through what I did, I welcomed the opportunity to put things in perspective. I decided to focus on God. I have been crying good cries and having great prayer sessions. Life has taught me where to place my priorities. I have learned a lot. I have become involved in an empowerment group in Atlanta. It is a group of women who come together and talk about real life situations. When I tell my story, others are inspired by what I have said and are encouraged to talk. My finances are thriving, I bought a house with cash. I am putting myself into many projects that align with my goals. I am working on boutiques and starting services for the homeless population with two others from my church. I am excited and I am nurturing myself from the inside out.

Chapter 3: Love of a Father

I had no examples in my life of what it was like to be loved by a man. Love was something I wanted, but I didn't know how to get it. I didn't have a male figure in my life to compare my father with. What he was giving wasn't love. My father was the type of man who rather hang out with his friends than spend time with his family. He would go to work at 6:00am in the morning and not come home until it was late in the evening. It seemed like the neighborhood was more appealing than us. My father didn't even try to build a relationship with his wife, let alone his girls. He did the basics of his responsibility as a provider, he provided food and shelter, and that was his limit.

A child wants to feel they are loved from their parents. Growing up we could show no emotion and there was no display of emotion shown to us, except anger and disappointment. Kisses on the cheek, a word of congratulations or I'm proud of you, we received none of that. I'm hands on with my kids. I tell them I love them and assure them that I am there for them. Refusing to allow my kids to go through the things my sisters and I went through I intentionally create an environment for them to be expressive. They are learning how to show emotions and express their feelings. We have conversations and facetime; our interactions have value for them and me.

Being hard on children can push them out into the world without a sense of direction. All they are seeking is to be accepted and loved. That was the experience for my sisters and me. I was 14 years old sneaking out of the window to hang with my girlfriends. We lived a life of sneaking around. My mom didn't pay attention to us either. We didn't have a relationship with her because she was preoccupied with my father.

Caught Outside

We were the kids in the neighborhood that had to stay in the house when our parents would leave. I still don't understand how our parents could be so strict with everything, loving us and not allowing us to be free to have fun. We did as we were told. We went to school and when we got home, we did our homework. I would think that doing that would earn us something. Being the cool kids in the neighborhood my sister and I figured out a method where we could still talk to our friends. It helped that everyone lived on the same street.

Sometimes we would talk to our friends through the window. Other times we would go outside and talk to them. Our system worked most of the time. We had friends that would watch out for our parents. They would tell us when they would leave and watch to see when they returned. The routine was that we would run back into the house before they could know the difference. One day, someone wasn't on their post. Our system failed that day

One day my parents went out for some reason. The signal came that we could come out. There we were outside having fun until my parents came and we were caught outside. We didn't have time to get back into the house. My father came up and slammed me against the brick. The kids watched in horror as he berated and pushed me into the house. I couldn't imagine the thoughts that were going through their minds. It was certainly no secret how rough and tough he was. Even when I am upset with my kids, they still know I love them. It's not that I was so surprised that my father would do such a thing. I had experienced abuse from him before. It was just more evidence of the extreme anger in him towards me. That day my friends witnessed it.

At school the next day, one of the boys asked if I wanted him to kill my father. In a strange way I appreciated that he said that. I felt like someone really cared. It proved that people do pay attention and can empathize with terrible situations. Killing my father wasn't the solution, I knew he wanted to help in the only way he knew how. I told him no. It was okay. "We're used to it."

I try my best to push those feelings to the side that make me angry or sad. Sometimes the feelings just appear. Once I reached a certain age, I blocked out a lot of things. Everyone that grew up in that house has a mental disturbance from the experiences. There are many things that I don't want to remember. I do have one fond memory where we went to a friend's house. It was nice because we could engage more intimately as a group of friends. Many of us were like brothers and sisters. It was the most fun we had as teens.

My Mother

My grandmother had six children; my mother was the oldest. My mother had the responsibility of taking care of all her siblings because her mother was always in the street. As an adult, I tried to understand what it was like to be a mother that didn't have a role model. I realized that my mother didn't have the capacity to give us more. She didn't have the example of a mother. Therefore, she couldn't model it for me. It takes the will to do something different than you experienced. I also believe that the mothering instinct should kick in. For me, I knew I didn't want my kids to have the same experience as I did, so I intentionally raised them a different way.

There was a time in my life when I desperately needed my mother. It was around the age of 14. Not only did I need her love, I needed her instruction. I wonder now if she would have been able to offer me any. There was one boy he was 17. He told me all that I wanted to hear. I had never heard the things he told me before. He told me how pretty I was. I was only 14. That age when girls get curious about the opposite sex. I liked the attention. I feel a father or mother should be the first to tell their daughter how pretty she is, maybe it won't be so shocking to hear when someone else says it. I never had the talk with my mother or father about how boys would approach you or what to watch out for. This boy talked with me like he wanted to be more than friends. I had met him a couple of times. According to him we were dating. Little did I know how thrown to the wolves, unprepared, and not taught any different I was.

My first experience with sex was at the age of 14. It took place in the house we all would hang out at. I ended up pregnant and was able to hide it for four months. My goal was to keep my parents from taking my baby from me. But they found out and forced me to have an abortion. I held a lot of anger toward my mom because she ran and told my father. Before the abortion, my father attempted to beat it out of me with a broomstick. That incident convinced me that I was leaving and never coming back.

Chapter 4: Finding My Father

My sister and I were waiting anxiously for the magical age of 18. It was the time, we thought we could finally get away from the abusive atmosphere for good. My sister had a boyfriend that told her that she could move out and move in with him. When she took him up on his offer my father called the police to get her back. I overheard the conversation the police had with my father when they arrived at our home. They informed him that they could not do anything because she was of age. I could only imagine how my sister felt, being on her own at last. I tried to patiently wait my turn.

When I turned 17, I started throwing my things into my bag. I felt it was time to make my exit. My mom thought I was just going to a friend's house. I told her I wasn't coming back.

"Why are you leaving?" She said.

I know she didn't want to be there by herself. The abuse we experienced would then shift back to her. Every feeling that my father had, anger, disappointment, his dominance would transfer again to her.

Despite my mom's questioning I left home and stayed with some friends here and there. I would get stopped by people who asked whether I was related to the Elliott. I had no clue who they were talking about.

I heard about what was going on at my home after I left. My father was never home until nighttime. My mom would stay in her room. She received orders to clean or perform other household chores, but she was not engaged because my mom was going through her own hell. When I saw my mom, I would ask her about it. Her response would be, "Baby, don't pay them any attention." But I knew things were bad. I also knew there was nothing I could do.

I learned about my biological father when I was 17 years old. But my mom was not the one to break the news to me. My aunt says that my mom was raised in the same church as he was. That's how she knew him. When the church family found out who my mother was, they were shocked. The picture started to come together. I asked my aunt about the name Elliott. My aunt responded by telling me to get in the car.

When we stopped driving, she said, "This is where your biological father stayed. I'm tired of your mother lying to you."

I walked up to the door. An older man came to the door.

"I think you are my father." The words felt strange coming out of my mouth.

"No, baby, you must be talking about my son."

I told him who I was, but he seemed to already know who I was. "Come on in, Baby," he said inviting me into his home. I was 20 when I wrote the first letter to my biological father. No one knew that I was aware of the secret that had been hidden from me while growing up. I hid it from age 17 to 36. It weighed on me for years. I didn't want to cause any more friction in my mom's household. My older sister was the one that told my mom that I knew. She told my mom that I went and found a man named Aaron and was saying that it is my biological father.

Confronting Mother

I was sitting in my living room one day when my mom came to my house banging on the door. She was in rare form. "Your sister told me that you went and found this man," was the first thing that came out of her mouth. "They have never done anything for you," was the next point she brought to my attention. I was shocked because at that moment she launched into a tirade about those people and what they hadn't done. She continued for a full two minutes straight. I felt her fear and desperation. There was nothing she could do. I knew the truth. My response flowed out like water. "So, now you are admitting it. You are saying that they have done nothing for me, but you didn't give them the chance to. They couldn't get to know me or anything." My mom was probably not expecting that kind of response, but all I felt was relief. I was relieved because she admitted it. I wasn't angry. But I was frustrated that I did not have the chance to confront her with it first.

Later, I found out that my mom and sister had got together and discussed the news without me. It seemed that their relationship was different when they were all together. My sister never told me that she was going to tell my mom. I told her the day my aunt took me to my grandfather's house. My mom had no response. She stormed out of the house so, I left it alone. I never talked to my mom about my new family. I held it for about 12 years. I knew that it was a sore spot that I would not profit from.

During the time that I found out about my biological father, my mother didn't know that I was spending time with my other family and getting to know them, I felt like I had to hide it. I would go by my grandfather's house or visit the church service. They were always happy to see me. I was that lost child that they knew about but couldn't find. I found out that I went to school with some of my aunts and uncles. We would pass each other in the hall not knowing that we were related. It made me upset. I realized that I had a crush on a guy who turned out to be my cousin. I could have ended up dating him without knowing that he was my family. That bothered me.

Meeting Virtually

I didn't meet my father right away because he was incarcerated in Miami, Florida. I wrote him a letter and told him who my mother was and that I was supposed to be his daughter. He never denied me. I never found out the full story of how he ended up in jail. I have been told by relatives that he had a really high IQ. I guess he was too smart for his own good. His story checked out to be true. He was incredibly smart.

My existence made sense every time I learned more about how I came to be. My father gave dates, times, and events about his correspondence with my mother. He set about to fill in the missing pieces for me. Six pages with times my mother snuck me to see him were filled out with details. When I read the letter, all I could do was smile. He filled in the pieces of the puzzle. He also filled an emptiness in my heart. It was strange to hear my father say he loved me. He told me how he was waiting on me to find him. Not wanting to cause any trouble in my home, all he could do was wait patiently. I understood,

I was 21. In 1998, my father wrote letters to me, but I had not received them because I moved. That's when he wrote to my uncle to get in contact with me.

In 2010 I got a call from my father. He was on the phone with my uncle at the time and I found out he had been released from prison. I was overwhelmed with happiness. I was excited for the opportunity to see him. We would talk every day throughout the day. It was like he was attempting to catch up on all the time he had missed. My father told me how beautiful I was. I couldn't understand it, it sounded so foreign to me. He would never get off the phone without saying he loved me, and he would not allow me to get off the phone without saying I loved him. Once, I got off the phone so quick, he called right back and said, "Let's do this again. You didn't tell me you loved me." I was not used to a man telling me he loved me, not even my husband. I certainly was not used to reciprocating it. It was something I had to get used to.

Section II: Meeting My Father

Chapter 5: Leaving

The first time I left home was 14. It was after I was forced to have the abortion. A girlfriend of mine took me in. Leaving home at such a young age and staying with a friend wasn't the ideal situation, but it gave me a sense of relief. In a perfect world, I could things working out differently for me. At that time, I was just responding to the pain I felt. I wasn't thinking about what my decisions would cost me further down the road.

During that time, I was questioned about my relationship with the Elliott family. People must have known something that I didn't. Often, I would get asked about my family and hear other people's story. So many different situations. Some people's experiences were worse than mine. I was dealing with physical and emotional abuse since I was a little girl. Being away from home made me feel a sense of freedom and relief. I had a peace of mind. No longer when I was trying to sleep did I have to hear yelling in my ear. My rest was peaceful. Little did I know that the restrictions that I was running from I would restrict myself in ways I couldn't fully understand at the time.

Pregnant

My girlfriend had another border who lived with her when I arrived. He was tall, dark, and handsome with the ability to always made me laugh. He had a strong male presence. I was soon taken by what I saw and how he made me feel. We began to date. My experience level with the opposite sex had not expanded. I was still young and didn't know much of anything about sex and relationships. My abortion experience was not followed with any education about understanding the opposite sex or how to have standards for yourself. My new boyfriend seemed to have more experience than me, in a way that made me feel safe.

There I was attracted to this guy and didn't know much about him at first. He was always gone in the streets. I didn't know what he did for money early in our relationship. I had no worries at that point, I wasn't working, just hung around my friend. She made sure I was okay. School wasn't a part of my daily routine because I dropped out in the 9th grade. After becoming more serious with my boyfriend, I was eating a lot. I recognized the same pattern from when I was 14. I soon realized that I was pregnant. He told his mom. She became a strong presence in my life. Without her, I don't know where I would be. My son was her first grandchild. She did a lot for me, took me to doctor's appointments, gave me money, and constantly called to see if I was okay.

A dark cloud cast its shadow right after I found out I was pregnant. My boyfriend was incarcerated. He did not meet his son until his 2nd birthday. He apologizes all the time for not being there. I ended up going to Job Corp when my son was 2 months old. His grandmother my boyfriend's mom kept him while I was gone. After a while I was got homesick for my baby so, I didn't complete the program. I needed to take a break from everything. My mind needed time to settle, so much had happened. I was at a standstill concerning the direction of my life, but I made sure to hold on to whatever peace I had.

I encountered a surprise when I returned from Job Corp, my friend no longer had the apartment. It was a hard decision but moved back in with my mother and father. My parents seemed to be okay with the grandchild I brought with me. They were completely different with interacting with grandchildren than they were with us as children. We couldn't do things when we were younger. I didn't allow them to give advice. I would tell them, "You didn't do a good job with us. I can't allow you to tell me how to raise my kids."

That living situation didn't last long. My son's father's mom offered to take in my son. I went and stayed with my older sister for a while. I was working at the time. My goal was to find myself and to get my life together. Soon I was able to get my own apartment. I didn't immediately move my son in with me. Back then, it seemed disruptive to remove my son from a stable environment. I saw him often. His grandma and I did the lion share of raising him. I am proud of that decision. He stayed with his grandmother in a positive area. My nephew was shot and killed in the environment where I stayed. My son has never been involved in the streets. His grandmother lived in the country. He was able to focus on schoolwork and growing up.

Marriage

My life took an even different turn after having my son and things not working out with me and his father. I had started working at a McDonalds, when my future husband walked through the door. I didn't know it at the time though. He wasn't my type, but he asked for my number. So, I gave it to him, thinking I would try someone different. He was short and muscular. I was used to men who were taller than me. But he was funny, and that caught my attention. My son was 5 or 6 years old at that time. This guy had a job which was different too. I had never dated a man with a real job. He worked in construction laying pipeline across the state making good money. It made me feel like something was wrong with me because he withheld money from me though he had plenty of it. I lost myself. Again, I found myself looking for something and not able to distinguish who or what it was.

He was a heavy drinker when I met him. I didn't think anything of it at the time. He would have alcohol in one hand and beer in the other. We would spend a great deal of time together. As a result, I got pregnant by him with my second son. That's when I found out that he was still in a relationship with a woman who also bore him children. I heard him on a 3-way call one day with her denying my son. I told him I didn't want to see him again. He left and I refused to answer his calls. After having my son his best friend came to visit me. When he looked in my son's face, he called his friend right away.

"This is your child! You need to come down here."

Though I didn't have anything to do with him, I was still connected with his friends. He visited me and brought the woman he was involved with along. I guess they both wanted to see for themselves if my son resembled him. I gave him the choice of being with his son or staying in that situation. He chose to come and live with me. My son was his first son. I think that played a role in his decision. At any rate I was happy because I had my son and my son had a father. Otherwise, there wasn't a lot of joy for me.

All the while we were living together, he was a womanizer and he cheated constantly. When he would stay out, he always had excuses. He was still fooling around with other women. He was often drunk when he got home. All he was concerned about was what I cooked. I don't know why I asked for explanations, but I needed to know for myself. It became a tug of war seeing who could outsmart the other. I wanted the truth and he didn't want to get caught in his lies.

Things seemed to change with each son I had. By the second son, the situation was worse. He denied that son as well. I didn't matter that we were living together, and I was only with him. The decision for us to get married came from an ultimatum I gave him. If he wasn't going to stop cheating, I was going to leave and take my children with me. I found myself being like my mother and accepting things in his behavior that was damaging me. I told him, "You don't have any intention of doing right by me. You don't even think of being married." A couple of days later he suggested that we get married. I believed he married me so I would not take the kids. It wasn't about me. I didn't believe it was happening until we arrived at the courthouse.

During that time, I was just happy that I had a real family. I did my best to dismiss the things that happened. I felt that he was at least putting effort into making things right. So, I was content with that. It never occurred to me that my self-esteem would take such a hit. I remember a couple of days before we got married, I talked to his mother. She asked me, "Are you sure you want to marry my son?" I should have taken that as a red flag along with many other red flags I had seen and ignored.

It wasn't until after we were married that I noticed the similarities between him and the father I grew up with. We look for men that are like our fathers, no matter how good or bad they are to us. I accepted things that I did not have to accept for the sake of wanting a real family. Because I am a nurturer, I was focused on caring for my family and creating a loving home despite the realities before me. Our marriage lasted 13 years. This was a season in my life that I held on to longer than I was meant to. He became a merchant seaman and worked on a few jobs out of state. He eventually began to work locally and continued to work on ships until he became too sick to work. My husband died August 14, 2018.

The Box

The girl in the box was dealing with a lot. It became harder and harder to prevent the box from exploding. A lot had transpired pertaining to my marriage. My marriage was based on my husband not wanting me to take his kids. I wanted to believe that he cared for me at least a little. But it was apparent that he cared more for the kids. All I wanted my husband to do was to stop the cheating and be with me only. Cheating began a couple of months after we were married. It was apparent that he married me just so I would not take his kids.

When things got bad, I blocked it out. He would be gone for thirty days at a time. Sometimes I wouldn't know he was even home. I would find a number and call it to only find out that he was home and staying with another woman. It got to the point where I was suicidal, I took pills and once slit my wrists. Nothing worked. The 5-year-old girl in the box was screaming out for help. There were times where I would stay in my bed a lot. I was going through a depression, I felt completely alone. People would call to check on me. But I didn't want to talk because I was ashamed. I always considered myself a private person. My husband was still going away on the ship. When I would go out, people had no clue what was going on. I could look like a million bucks going to work or the grocery store. My husband was making over really good money each month, but he would not contribute to the household unless the children called and asked for money. Sometimes he would come home with nearly 20 phone numbers from women. Most of the women were people like me. I would call and talk to them and what I heard from them would send me into more of a depression.

I wanted to have a family so bad in a way, I was like my mother. I put up with things so that I could have a two-parent household for my children. I held on to that hope that things would eventually work themselves out. That grip almost drove me crazy. In the back of my mind I knew that I had to find a way to let go and take care of myself.

More tragedy came my way when my husband had a massive stroke while he was in New York. He had taken me off the bank account, so I had no money to get there. My sister purchased a plane ticket for me to get there. My husband's job took care of the cost of the hotel and my travel back and forth to the hospital. When I checked the bank account, he only had $300 in his account. He allowed other women to account for his money.

That experience with my husband made me wonder if something was wrong with me. He would not notice me. He would come home, and I would have my nails and hair done. But he didn't pay me any attention. I would pick him up and he would be in the house for maybe an hour before he felt the urge to leave. The he would not come back. I would get a call from him in the morning asking what I cooked for breakfast. I was devoted during his illness, I got there and nursed him back to health. His job was over after that. He knew that his time was coming to an end. He had days when he would feel better than others.

Chapter 6: Cooper's Bridge

Depression

The weight of my life was taking a toll on me beneath the surface. Everything from the time I was a young girl to the time I got married impacted the way I thought about myself. I remember thinking that leaving home was the answer. I would be away from the abuse from my father and the passive reaction of my mother. After leaving home trouble seemed to be disguised as something appealing at first, then things would end up either hurting me or setting me back further from what I truly wanted. I knew that I wasn't equipped to deal with everything I was going through. Confidence and self-esteem were not modeled or taught at my house. No one encouraged you that you were special and should achieve something. Most sadly I didn't have a father who loved his wife in such a way that her daughter would see that love and only accept that kind of love from other men.

When I got married, I tolerated the abuse and neglect my husband handed out. I never saw any of it coming when we first met. If I had known that I would have to drive around with a bat in my car because of the women my husband had encounters with, I would have had second thoughts about being with him. He would concoct stories that convinced these women of extraordinary things. By the time they encountered me, they were incensed at what they saw as the evil I was perpetrating on a good man. I was the wife having to defend our relationship from the lies he constructed to woo these women.

I sunk into a depression. My depression was displayed in my behaviors and thought process. I isolated myself. There was no desire to be around people. My thoughts were damaging to me mostly. I felt like I wasn't good enough. Whatever I did, it wasn't good enough. I began to doubt myself. All of this was in the light of me feeling like I am a strong woman. I found my strength in taking care of people. It took the focus off what I was experiencing. Though I went into my shell, I never changed what I wanted. There was a way that I wanted to experience love. I didn't know what depression was then. But today I recognize the signs and symptoms I exhibited.

The Dream

It was really happening. I took my phone and drove in my car to the bridge. I placed my phone in the holder and recorded my life story. The 5-year-old girl in the box could not care for me any longer. The pressure had become too great for her. I discussed what was happening. I talked about my hurt and my despair. I left messages for my kids and other loved ones and I asked for their forgiveness. I told them that I loved them. I left the phone recording and walked out of the car and jumped.

I woke from the dream in a panic. Immediately reached for the phone and called friends that I had not talked to in a while. I expressed that I needed help. My whole life, I have not been comfortable asking for help. It was huge that I took that step. I felt as if I needed to die to wake up and get the help I needed.

Going through depression and being suicidal, can lead to death. In my dream, I felt alone. My life was in major overload. I was intentionally distant from friends and family. People were calling and checking in, but I kept to myself. I was the type of person that kept things to myself. Only a few friends and family knew about my struggle.

The thought about suicide was present throughout my life. I didn't feel wanted from my parents or feel loved from my husband. I would cut my wrists, but I didn't cut deep enough to follow through with suicide. I only cut deep enough to feel some other type of pain. My friend already knew what I was going through mentally with my husband. What he didn't know was the seriousness of clinical depression. When I told him that I dreamed of jumping off the bridge, he was shocked. He knew that I was afraid of heights and water.

My friend couldn't help, that was the reality. Other people were going through things as well. Some were going through depression and didn't know it. Today, I have five friends who have been medically diagnosed with depression. It's a real tragedy. When I began to express my truth and what I was feeling and how I was processing, they found that they were in need as well. I was going through it with my husband. They were going through it in other ways. I was the one that others would call to talk through their problems with. Carrying my own depression along with hearing how my friends were struggling may have sent me into emotional overload.

Wishing I Had a Brother

When I found out that I had a brother, I was so excited to get to know him. I really wanted a relationship with my brother. The 5-year-old girl who was being abused wanted an older brother to protect her. Those were my exact words when I was a little girl. Though it wasn't what I thought it would be, I was grateful. My brother was not the type to talk on the phone. He would text. My heart grew knowing that I had him. I reached out to my brother and told him things that were going on in my life. He would send me motivational quotes. My need for a brother made me concerned with wanting to hear his voice and to know how he felt about me. I needed a strong male in my life that genuinely cared about me.

I sent my brother a long text message telling him that I was suicidal. In the text I explained that I knew that he was going through things himself. But I stressed that I needed to talk to him. He knew the relationship between me and my husband. I needed to hear his voice and talk to him. Within five minutes my brother called me.

The conversation we had was like that I had with the counselor. His words were therapeutic. I wanted to hear more. He told me to be strong. "Don't allow others to get you to a place where you don't want to live anymore," is what he told me. What he was saying was not new to me. Going through my depression, I heard a lot of things like that. I wanted to hear more. There had to be more that came after that. In his own way he was supportive.

As I got older, I continued to long for a strong male presence in my life. I wanted a connection. My brother still texts, which is his way of communicating. I have accepted the relationship as it is. I must release the yearning of wanting to know him more. It seems that every man in my life doesn't work out. Maybe it has something to do with what my expectations are. I have realized that everything I have wanted in a man is available in God. I must give myself to him and look to him to provide the presence I crave.

Sometimes during my prayers, I must stop and chastise myself. I'll be praying for God to send me someone to love me unconditionally, to protect me, and care for me. Then I would realize that I was describing God. I must practice seeking God first to provide what I need.

Two Days

I tried counseling thinking it would help me heal. The counselor was questioning me about my marriage. I said I was married but didn't know what it felt like to be married. She responded that she had never heard that before. I made the decision not to go back. When I spoke to her, I didn't get a sense of relief. Talking with her was like talking with someone who didn't have a degree. It was like talking to someone out on the street. She was shocked by what I was saying and told me things that I already knew. My goal was to get an understanding about what I was going through. She had nothing insightful to say. When I told her that I was just a secretary, maid, and caretaker in my marriage, she didn't seem to understand. I tried to explain how I wanted more than the title of being a wife, I wanted to have a relationship. I only had a title. I wanted to hear more about something she couldn't provide. First impressions truly do matter.

I finally got the nerve to leave and we separated. Trying to heal on my own in my own way became the path I took. I remember when I went to my doctor. He asked, "How are you feeling?" I broke down.

I didn't know what else to do. My primary care physician placed me on medication. That was his way of helping me. I had been taking care of my husband for years. Even though we were separated, I would drop everything and go to take care of him every time he would call not feeling good. When he would push me away, I would leave. One weekend, I was down taking care of him. I took him to the doctor. Once the doctor would give him the all clear, his attitude changed. He suddenly didn't like me or need me anymore.

On my drive from Charleston to Georgia on the weekend, I was praying so hard that I felt the Holy Ghost moving in my body so distinctly. That was the beginning of me being led to where I needed to be intentionally, practically, tangibly. My leg could not stop moving.

This experience and what happened next led me to become a praying woman. One day I was on my machine working. Something told me to go home. I was just there on the weekend. It was Wednesday. I did not listen. I went home. I got up the next morning and went to work. I lasted for a couple of hours before the voice was so strong that I could not resist it. Four hours I drove to take care of him. My son greeted me at the door with a smile. When I walked into my husband's room, he greeted me with a smile as well. That was unusual. He never did that. I was there for about a week. During that time, my husband and I had a chance to talk. He told me that he appreciated everything I had done for him. I felt a true feeling of relief. I never felt that he appreciated me.

Before I left, he complained that his legs and arms were hurting. We went to the hospital. He received morphine for pain. The morphine caused his breathing to speed up. After getting checked out and seeing that his blood work was fine, he was sent home. By the time he was in the car my husband started hallucinating. He told me he was afraid to walk up the stairs of the home. He was in so much pain. I told him I love him. Despite what he put me through, I really did love him. Back to the hospital again, this time he had to be sedated and placed on a breathing machine. It was a hard sight to see, his body was swelling with fluids. I was told that I had a decision to make, a decision to pull the plug. My husband died two days later. Because he had a pacemaker, they had to wait until his heart stopped beating completely. I sat and held his hands until his heart stopped.

I am grateful that God gave me the opportunity to spend that time with my husband. He knew that my husband could not go through it alone. I got on my knees and prayed to God to take me instead of him. Regardless of my treatment at the hands of my husband, I would give my life for his. All this time, I wanted my husband. But I could not have him fully. Even when he was sick and fragile, he still was dealing with other women. They didn't care that he was sick, they just wanted his money. I was the only woman taking care of him. I lost jobs to take care of him. When he called, I had to go. Being a wife, I felt obligated to do what I could for him. Some have said that I wasn't obligated, but my heart is too big for that. I took the pain and abuse. I accepted the backlash and mistreatment and still took care of him. If I had not learned to pray, I would really be a mess. I felt like God had me go through this to make me the strong woman that I am today. I wanted to hear that he appreciated me and cared for me. It wasn't until the funeral that his mom told me about his hidden thoughts. He told her that he liked to get me upset and see my response. He liked the passion in my responses because it showed that he was loved. He also often confided in her that he appreciated everything that I did for him. I needed to hear it, but he was incapable of telling me until the end.

There are times when I still deal with the pain. I want to release the pain, but I know I must own it first. God is educating me on how to use it as growth. He knows that I am stronger than what I thought I was. I knew growing up that I would be a powerful speaker. He is preparing me for that. He has surrounded me with people that are teaching me what I need to know. My journey has been about more than my pain though I haven't always seen it that way.

Church has been a place where I felt I could be fed. I went to one church but realized that I couldn't eat from that table. I would go in one way and leave the same way. So, I tried another church. A speaker asked if someone would like to receive the Holy Ghost. I went forward and felt what seemed like a panic attack. I went into prayer the next day and found myself crying for myself. I am no longer that 5-year-old in the box. I was recently rebaptized. I am preparing myself for what is to come. I must open myself up and allow the holy spirit to work on me. At times, I would attend my grandfather's church. He was a bishop. Water rushed from my feet to my head. I ran out of the church. I have continued to open myself up. When the water rushes, it is my release and I'm learning to live within him. I have been the one stopping that process. I went through what I went through. I feel that I had to go through that. Now, I am motivated and eager to grow. I am excited to learn more. That is what makes me happy.

Chapter 7: Letting Go of Father

My biological father had a custom of calling me in the morning. One morning, he called but something was different about this call, it was heavy. He said he had something to tell me. He had gone to the doctor and found out that he had cancer, stage III. All that time in prison and he never knew that he had cancer. He had only been out three months. That was also all the time we had was three months. It felt like I was being stabbed in my stomach. I started crying. I had just received the gift of my father in my life and I was not ready to let him go.

There he was trying to comfort me by telling me it was going to be okay. That he was strong and was going to fight it. I was in a confused state of mind. I questioned God. It was hard for me to understand how could lose him. I was finally loved unconditionally by a man. He was the father that I wished for. In the short time that we had known each other he had become a vital part of my life. I was shaken.

At this point, I knew my sisters and brother. I had searched for them for years. We initially had communicated with each other before my father was released from prison. I found them on Facebook and sent them both the same message. The older of the two sisters got in touch with me. I met my brother the year he was drafted to the Washington Wizards, I would call and never get an answer. We spoke one time before I met him in person. My older sister welcomed me. She did not push me away. She is nurturer like I am.

My younger sister and I became closer over time. We built a bond. We hang out when we have time. We are both Sagittarius and have a lot in common along with her only being a couple of days younger than me. I feel more connected to them than with my mother's children. I thank God every day for giving me more siblings.

Hospital Visit

When my father took a turn for the worse, I reached out to them. I relayed the message that I received, "I was told to let you know that dad caught pneumonia on top of the lung cancer. I was told to let you know that our brother was taking the next flight out there." It was like they didn't want to have much to do with my father. I am the type to find peace in situations. I felt that if they knew he was dying, they could see the opportunity to find some closure. My older sister ended up driving to Miami with her husband. She had the opportunity to speak with him when he was released to a nursing facility. I don't know what they talked about, but I hope she found closure.

My brother flew directly to Miami. He arrived before I did with one of my aunts that was already there. My nerves were fraught. I was overwhelmed that I was meeting my brother and father at the same time. I saw a tall guy come out of my father's room. He pulled me in the room. I met my brother that I have always wanted and my father at the same time. I stood paralyzed.

I smiled. Then, I cried. I saw a man lying in the hospital bed looking like me. I saw myself. My eyes, my lips, my cheekbones, everything. I had my own unique look growing up. I always felt different. My features were different from my sisters, my mother, and the father I grew up with. When I examined his face, I knew where I came from. He beckoned me forward. He hugged me and I cried. I was no longer lost. Every bit of my face was his face. It was as if he spit me out as they say. I didn't know why my mom felt like I did not need to know my background and where I came from.

We stayed and visited together for a while. My brother had not seen my father since he was a little kid. My younger sister, my brother, and I, he left all of us. He had not seen us since we were little. When he received his diagnosis, we were all in our 30s. A relationship needed to be built between a father and his kids. I was able to see the relationship between my father and my brother building right in front of me. My brother opened his heart and they talked like they had always been a team. My father did not think he would get that opportunity. He was grateful. It was a sight to see. I watched them together, they were two of a kind sharing the same mannerisms and distinctive laugh. They connected instantly. I made one other trip back to visit.

The Loss

My father and I kept in touch from June 2010 to Thanksgiving morning that same year. I visited him two times during that time. I was grateful for every conversation I had and the time I got to see him. Before I received the most dreadful phone call ever, I had been calling my father a few times and getting no answer. I thought he had gone out to visit friends. Later, I got the dreadful news.

While I was sitting in the car at my mother's house with my kids on Thanksgiving Day my aunt called. She told me that my father had lost consciousness and was rushed to the hospital. My kids knew something was wrong. They didn't have a relationship with the father I grew up with. They had more of a relationship with my biological father. When they saw me crying, they began to cry as well. My mother walked toward the car as I was crying. She asked what was wrong. I told her. "Well what do you want me to do?" That was her immediate response. She was upset that I was building the relationship with my biological father. She still had not told my stepfather that I knew.

The whole ride down to see my father, I kept telling myself that he was okay. I prayed and hoped that I would arrive, and he would be awake. My wish was that I would be able to say to him what I have said many times before. I wanted to tell him that I loved him. That I was there for him. But by the time I arrived in Miami, he was sedated. I didn't get to talk to him again.

I walked into the room and witnessed his still body lying in the bed. I stroked his hand and his hair which had turned white. Speaking to him as though he could hear me, I told him that I was thankful for the chance to know him. My feeling was that he was already gone but I stayed until it was time leave. I realized that there was nothing else that I could have done. I felt a sense of closure. He was on life support for two weeks. My aunt did not want to take him off. We just had to wait until she thought it was time.

The funeral was beautiful, but I felt numb. I stood and gave the story of our communication. I had them laughing about his insistence on saying I love you. I voiced my gratitude for the fact that he filled a hole in my heart that I had held for years. I appreciated the opportunity to experience unconditional love. Never one to stand up and speak in front of people, I found myself needing to speak for him. He looked so good in the casket that I felt peace. I cherished the six months we shared.

Section III: Loving Myself

Chapter 8: Finding Myself in Loss

When I looked over what my life had been with my parents and husband, I realized it was time for a change. So much of my time was caring for others. Though I was struggling to heal myself, I put others first. I looked around one day and there I was trying to pick up what pieces of myself was left. I watched two men in my life die. I lost out on a childhood that could of went a different way if I was loved a different way. I didn't have the best relationship with the sister I grew up with. In the quiet space of my mind, I had to ask, "Who am I?" I looked in the face of the three boys given to me by my husband and I thought, I am their mother. But, somewhere deeper in my being I knew there was more. How much longer was the 5-year-old girl in the box to remain there?

Having the opportunity to meet my biological father was good for me. It helped me identify where I came from and experience the love

I was missing from a father. Now I must put all the pieces together from my experience and unbury my whole self. I feel that God is challenging me now, "What are you going to do?" I have learned that I must step back and create and that meant time to think and care for myself in a holistic way.

Finding Myself

The more I take care of myself and grow, the less I see of the 5-year-old girl. She and I continue to grow into the full-grown woman that I knew I could become. The 5-year-old girl has been released from the box. It hasn't been easy, but I am learning to be proud of myself. There are things that I didn't think I could handle on my own. The future holds many new beginnings for me. I must put my big-girl pants on so I can take hold of them.

To know myself fully I had to experience what I did. I now know what I'm made of. It was not in vain. The love I gave to my sick husband who only cared that I was there when he needed me. Then showed his displeasure for me when he was well, was not in vain. At any moment I could of turn and ran never to return. But I continued to share what was in me. I can still remember clearly when I was at work in Georgia. The voice I heard telling me to go home. I hauled tail to South Carolina. When I knocked on the door, my son and my husband was smiling. A week and a half later, he was having leg and back pain. I took him to the emergency room. I was there the whole time from the time he had the major stroke in New York until the end.

I still talk to my husband today. It is not different from the way I talk to God. I do it with a smile on my face. That's my way of healing. I tell him that I have it from here. I applaud what he had done in raising his kids. I feel confident to know that I can do what my husband left and what God wants me to do. It wasn't easy raising boys on my own most of the time. My husband was gone a lot. When he was around, he would undermine my authority. It got to the point where my youngest boy got physical.

When my baby boy graduated, I cried for myself and my husband. My husband's death did not only affect me but his youngest son too. My youngest boy has some anger issues. We got into an altercation that broke me. I have walked around on eggshells ever since. He flipped out. Dealing with my son is a new situation. He recognizes he needs help. I recognize that what happened between me and my husband could cause our boys to feel a way. I myself was at a crossroad when he died. All I had been doing for so long was taking care of him, so it was all I knew how to do. I had to learn to put one foot in front of the other and keep it moving.

At one time there was a black cloud over me. The largest percentage of the stress was from my marriage. Soon I began to take responsibility for many things. I had to find that I was stronger than I thought I was. My friends thought I was strong because I was able to endure what I was going through. But I didn't feel that way. I could feel the weight on my shoulders, but I didn't feel the strength to hold it. I was taking care of both my parents and my husband. My life was on hold. Anything that I wanted to pursue would have to be dropped. That was then. Things had to change.

I have learned that I must step back and create the situation where people are not so dependent on me. It is working out. Placing myself as first, calls other family members and friends to duty. For example, with my parents. Family members have come to help me and take care of the needs of my parents. I no longer must fight through it from my sense of obligation. I am better when I do help because I have taken care of myself. The next move I made was to shut friends and family off so I could concentrate and focus on what was next. I moved back to Georgia. It took me about three months to sort it out through prayer and solitude.

The Process

Finding myself was a process that involved loving myself, focusing, and pushing through the pain. I want to share that process with others that may be facing their own challenges in life. I won't tell you it's easy but if you can work through each point you will gain some wisdom.

Loving Yourself is number one. Nothing comes without self-love. I have loved everyone and kept forgetting myself. When I learned to love myself, I found the focus to do what I needed to do and the courage to push through. I found my strength in loving God first and then myself. Seeing and truly feeling his love for me allowed me to love myself. You cannot be happy until you love yourself.

Focus on what you want out of life. Know that there are things that you need to keep to yourself. Don't share everything that you are going to do with everybody. People didn't know that I was in the process of writing this book until it was published. I only told two people. I told them because they have my best interest at heart. They really want to see me prosper.

Pushing Through is critical. You will have people around you that will distract. People around you will not want you to accomplish something that they can't accomplish. What comes to you is for you. You must follow through on that. Don't allow others to steer your focus into the wrong direction. I came to realize that I was a strong woman whole time. I just couldn't see from being buried beneath the fear and pain.

Decline

Watching the people in my life decline in health wasn't easy. I literally witnessed the fight within them dissipate. There was something unsettling about it yet in the back of my mind I couldn't think of another outcome. My mother had a major stroke. Later, my husband had a stroke about one month after my mother. Then my father had a stroke right after that. The sequence of events kept me busy. I took care of my husband to his last heartbeat. No matter what goes on in life, death is final. After that there is no second chances to try and do something better. I gave him all I had to give, and I felt good about that.

During the time of watching my parents suffer, I intentionally put my pain in perspective. I was better regardless of what they put me through. What was important at that time was loving them unconditionally, the very thing I wanted. Everyone doesn't have the capacity to know what they want and then give it away not caring if it will be given back. I learned that there is a healthy way of doing that. It really is about your mindset and the way you see things.

I took the time to visit my parents. It was my attempt to I try to spend time with my mom and build a relationship with her. When talking with my mom I feel I can now speak openly about how I feel. Any questions of "Why" only result in her responding with, "It's your daddy." She was still in denial and unaware. When visiting, I pay their bills and do what I can. No one wants to come to their house because they created bad blood between relatives. My mom blames it on my father. I don't try to correct her or make her uncomfortable. I know cannot treat her poorly no matter how she has treated me. My love is conditional for her.   I give them both hugs when I leave, but I don't hold any illusions that there is anything other than the present. I am healed and I do what I do. My dad tells me that he appreciates me. My mom says thank you a lot. She can barely talk, but she manages to get that out. My parents have changed since me and my sisters have our own kids. He has a close relationship with my kids, but not with my sister's kids. My sister has told her kids about the past. I guess they will have to draw their own conclusions.

I have always been the type of person that puts other's needs ahead of mine. There was a time when my mother fell backward, and it overwhelmed me. I got into the shower and cried. When I'm in that space, it is a lot. It pushes me back to when I was taking care of my husband. I handle being overwhelmed with prayer. I face situations head on and pray.

No Coincidence

Things do happen for a reason. I haven't always known how to pray. There was certainly much to pray about. In 2010, my husband was getting sicker. It seemed at different points of my life there were things that needed to be dealt with. At one point I was having problems with my son. During the time that my husband was sick, every time he called, I went back. I had to do my part. I wanted my children to see me be there for their father.

There was a time during all that was happening that I went to live with a close friend. I don't feel like this was just a coincidence. She taught me something. At the time I was going through something with my son. I had to let it go. I had left at that moment and didn't go back. A really close friend taught me how to pray. She went through the house praying hard and loudly. I would leave the house trying to get away. After a while, I found myself walking through her house and praying. Now, I can pray. She often says, "Remember when you were anxious?" I had to go through that. I believe that was God's plan of equipping me. I have known that I was to be a motivational speaker. My grandfather was a bishop. I know this is what I am called to do.

Now that nothing is in my way, the sky is the limit. In the beginning I had some fear, but it went away quickly. The transition that I am going through now is to focus on myself. I used to focus on others and put them first. I am now developing myself. My outlook is brighter, I am starting my cleaning business. I wake up and smile every day. I am doing things for myself. How to care for myself was not something I was taught. I tried, but something always happened where I had to drop things and take care of someone else. The more I did I could see where to step toward bigger and better things. Writing this book is a demonstration of where my focus needs to be. I will be prepared to share my story and hopefully bless someone else. I now realize that I am supposed to do more.

Chapter 9: Deeper into God

You always seem to want the very thing you didn't have. Growing up I had a family and a father, but neither one was nurturing to me. The father that raised me didn't provide the love I needed, he abused me instead. My family was around me but, we were not together. The house that I grew up in was a house, not a home. My experience left me yearning for what I didn't have, a father who loved me and a family to call my own. I tried to have a family with my husband. We had the bare structure, but my husband was not committed, he chose to ignore me. When we separated, he would call me to do things while he was dating many women. I would tell him to ask one of them. He would say, "You are my wife. You are supposed to do this." When I said that I wanted a marriage that's not what I had in mind. I was more of a secretary than a wife. I wasn't a friend until toward the end. It started to be apparent that God had a purpose for my life, and he was preparing me for it. I would get the things I wanted but it wouldn't be the way I envisioned it.

Closer

God took me through experiences to strengthen me to be the woman he wants me to become. He gave me some time with my biological father because I wanted to feel that kind of love. My biological father was a blessing. My father growing up did not focus on his kids. I am only building that relationship now with the father that raised me because I am taking care of them. He knows he needs me now. That's the extent of our relationship. I never told my biological father that finding him was finding the piece of the puzzle that was missing in my life. I am grateful for the time I had with him even though it was short. I needed that opportunity. He filled a void for me. In a sense, I know what God was doing. I know now what it feels like to be loved. I can't complain. When I experienced that feeling of being loved by my father and his loss, I separated from my husband. I told myself that I was not going to accept anything less than what my father was showing me. I know the love I am worthy of.

I smile when I get an overwhelming feeling from God. This is the love I feel now. God's love is what kept me searching for more. I am experiencing the vastness of his love working in my life. When I put my focus on getting closer to God, I feel his presence more vivid in my life. He is enough. God is showing up in different areas of my life, I am still understanding how he works. There was a time I was driving with a friend of mine. I had a feeling that welled up on the inside of me. At the time I could only describe it as the something that started like a panic attack, but now I know it was God working with me.

I talk to God constantly. Prayer is something that is constant in my life. I know that he is drawing me closer to him. That calling on my life spoken and felt from my youth is still present. There was so much going on that I was absent from my calling. Now that my life has calmed down, I can focus on that. If you ever find yourself in that situation, search for peace. Sometimes it's hard to know how loud it is around until you get somewhere quiet. Search for space to listen, where you can open yourself to see God. The message I received about ministry came through meditation in that space.

Testing

I still have a lot of work to do on myself. I'm patient with the process. I have given enough time to situations that don't work, I want to give even more attention to what I know is working for me. There is a difference in how I do handle life. I know that I'm not alone. It's not me against the obstacles. I share my battles with God who fights them for me.

My faith is always being tested. But I have endured the attacks. For me to endure I had to first understand that the attacks only make me stronger. I didn't always know this, so my reaction was different. I would feel defeated or burdened down in those moments. Now, I wait for it. I act and don't run with fear. A good example is one time I went to sleep. Something told me to wake up. I felt a presence on the left side of my bed. It was like someone was coming onto my bed. I wasn't scared. Once I felt that presence, I felt held down, my body couldn't move. While I was being held down, I tried to pray but I could not speak or move. I began to pray hard in my mind. Then, I was released. I jumped up, and immediately ran downstairs to call my close friend. That situation made me stronger. I know there is a calling on my life and I believe that I will be a powerful speaker. I don't know when it will come, but I know it is coming. I anointed my whole house after that incident.

I have apostles and other leaders that support me. They guide me in the things I should be doing. I got rebaptized because of the attack. I am constantly listening to inspirational and gospel messages. Testing brings about strategies for me. I use the knowledge and the holy spirit to teach me. I am also learning to speak God's word. My path has been re-directed since I have been operating in who I am and who I am called to be.

Chapter 10: Finding My Peace

Loving myself was not something I always knew how to do. There was a time that I wouldn't even thought of that as something that I needed to do. I learned through my experience that blaming myself for things that happened in my life was a barrier to my own success. When I learned about God's love for me it helped me see that loving myself was important. There were so many spots in my life where I didn't feel complete, I felt like I needed so much. As much as I wanted to be loved completely no one could give that to me. When accepted God in my life things changed. The love I felt from God was overwhelming, it made me feel full. God's love is complete. When I communicate with God, I feel whole, he showers me with a love that covers all that I felt like I was missing. I know that others don't know this wholeness. I was one of those people once.

To explain the love that nurtured me to wholeness would require exploring the state of mind I was in at the time I felt lost. That would bring clarity to the process. Many can say that they understand, but have they experienced my situation? If someone were to reach me when I was in that space, they would have to connect with me while was giving. I have always been a nurturer. Caring for others came first. I couldn't resist offering help. I know now that it is my gift as well as a need. That is where learning about love has helped me. A lot of my time has been giving, but I didn't feel good about myself and I wasn't getting anything in return. Yet, it is in me to do even if I don't want to. When my husband didn't want me there, I had to be there. No matter how he sent me away, I had to come back. It is the same with my friends. My life is service.

I have always wanted to show love to others. No one would reciprocate love in the way I gave it. I have a friend that went to church with me once. She was going through hell in her life without any help other than from alcohol. She is the type of person who holds in things that are tearing her apart, while blaming herself for a lot of things just like I was. I told her that she must open to release the pain that is within her. I talked to her about it and she cried. She is learning to release and cry happy tears. My friend told me one time that she has never had anyone to listen, care, and allow her to release. It takes time, but she is learning.

The motivation for me was to give the love that I never had. I wanted to provide others with a sense of being loved. I wanted them to know that someone is there for them. I did not have anyone there for me. The need for someone to listen and tell you that it will be okay is all you need, sometimes. Just to be acknowledged is a win. I could relate to wanting to feel like I was somebody, that I had a purpose, or that there was a reason for me to here. It is the difference between life and despair. I felt like I was invisible, and no one noticed me. I had to realize that I mattered. For anyone reading this book, I want you to know YOU MATTER!

Love from Overflow

I am a bundle of love in my own eyes. My closest friends say the same. I am learning to give that love to myself. When I think of what I have learned about how God loves I can't help but think I could have loved more. God's love is so powerful that it overflows. It allowed me to love without wanting anything in return. I no longer had to wish for love from others. There was enough to love myself and give some to others in a more whole way. I wanted to cry for myself when I thought back at how I wanted to be loved so bad. Just to feel the love I gave in return, to be acknowledged and noticed seemed like a simple thing to want. Everything was bottled up in me and needed to be released.

When I finally released the pain and opened to love in a different way it was like that water flowing up from my toes to my head in my father's church. But the key was to get closer to God. I began to release the need that was pent up in the giving. I began to feel love for myself that was abundant and limitless. Instead of the love needing to come back and feed me, it has already done its work when I show it to others.

Love pushes. When you begin to love yourself, it pushes people away sometimes. My sister in my mom's home is one example. I was a tomboy growing up. When I had my first son is when I blossomed. My sister has a lot of hatred for me because we are different. She hates the woman that I am becoming. I look back and now and understand the struggles I had growing up better.

I decided to put myself first. When I realized that people in my life were using me or draining me, I had to separate myself from them. There is a difference between someone who needs help and those who want to use you. When my husband died, I had to cleanse my atmosphere. I had to let people go that were not healthy for me. Some were friends and some were family. Eventually I became more at peace with the decisions I made. Previously, I had always been the "Yes Girl." I had to learn to say no.

Love pulls as well. Love attracts people that are positive. I had one pastor tell me that I have a light over me. I am loved by so many people. People are drawn to me. They come up to me and speak life into me. People notice my better qualities and benefit from my advice. I am surprised when people repeat what I told them.

Attraction

There is a calling on my life. I know my calling is to speak with young adults, men and woman alike. I have not realized that men and women go through the same things. My desire is to travel and speak life to people. I don't know whether to call it ministry or motivational speaking, I think there is no difference between the two. The need I have for helping others through my speaking ministry is manifesting. I love meeting new people and engaging with them. Recently I applied for my passport. My plan is to travel and make people smile in other places of the world.

I am in a process of building my network by connecting with so many in my local community and abroad. I meet women in several women's groups that I am a part of. I am starting the process of handing out contact information and connecting with women who are doing several things. I am interested in being a blessing to all the populations represented in the women's groups. This includes women in

sex trafficking, homeless, mothers in poverty, and many other populations.

I must build myself up daily. I must engage to get people to
know me. I am competent in marketing. It is something that I will use
to develop myself further. I don't entertain cost or access as barriers.
My access to people is unfettered. Support is not a problem either. At
this point nothing can stop me from my calling. Writing this book is
something that no one expected me to do. It is the first step in sharing
the knowledge I have gained. I also want to take some classes to gain
more knowledge about what I want to do. My hope is that many will
read this book and find the answer to that "something about you" that
they see in me.

Lately, I have been watching YouTube videos of TD Jakes
daughter. I see myself doing the same thing she is doing. The Holy
Spirit has been teaching me so much that I am surprising myself. I
know that this is my platform. I see myself as a powerful mouthpiece.
When I see Cora Jakes Coleman, I see myself. I have a hunger for that.
My faith is increased knowing that I am worthy to do a good work.

I envision myself standing on a platform surrounded by many
spiritually motivated people that are making me stronger in what I
need to do. I tell myself it will happen. I am standing in the presence
of God being directed to do what I need to do. I am unstoppable. I
want to have the passion so built up in me that it flows off my tongue.

Prayer will give you peace and peace will give you strength to push through the past hurt. When you have peace within yourself then your hopes for a brighter future will come into existence.

Made in the USA
Columbia, SC
14 July 2020

13856341R00050